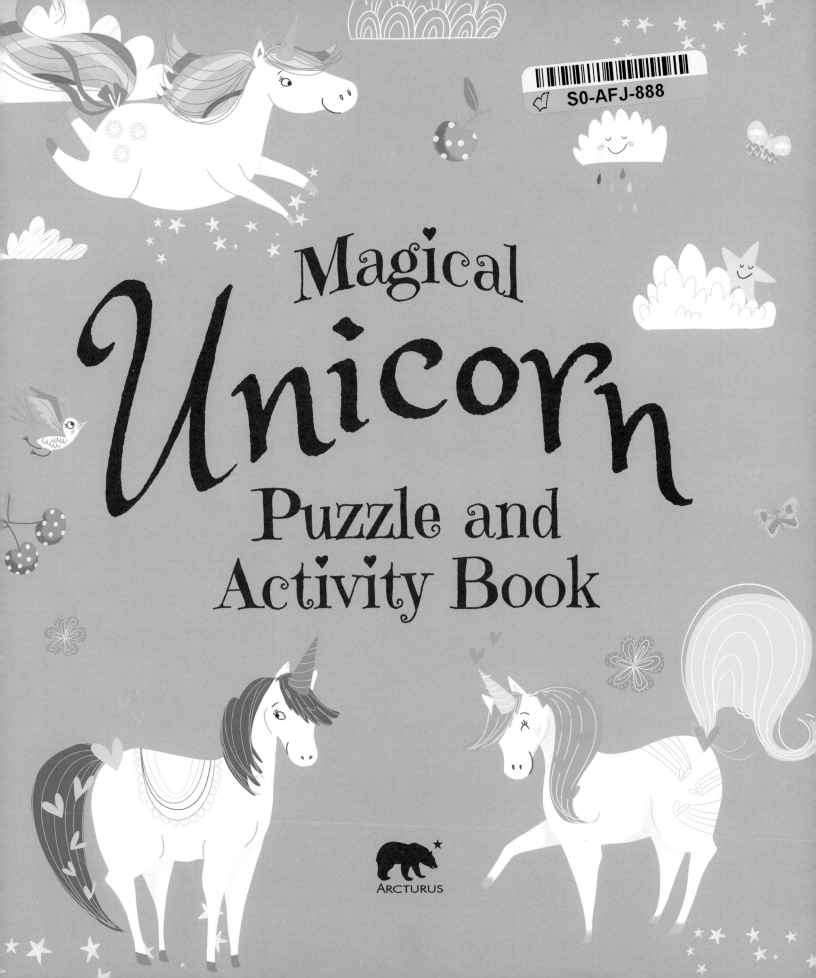

Magical Unicorn

Puzzle and Activity Book

ARCTURUS

ARCTURUS

This edition published in 2019 by Arcturus Publishing Limited
26/27 Bickels Yard, 151–153 Bermondsey Street,
London SE1 3HA.

Illustrated by Samantha Loman
Written by Sam Williams
Edited by Penny Worms
Designed by Well Nice Ltd

ISBN: 978-1-78950-466-8
CH006970NT
Supplier 29 Date 0119 Print run 7921

Printed in China

COME ON IN!

Welcome to a land of magic, where unicorns play in enchanted forests, fairies fly above cotton candy clouds, and mermaids splash in a pink lemonade sea.

There are ten unicorns playing hide-and-seek inside the royal castle. Can you find them all?

Prom Prep

Marigold is getting ready for her prom night.
Which of these silhouettes is an exact match for her?

4

Picnic Fun

Put this picture of Rosie and her fairy friends back together again.
Which piece doesn't fit anywhere?

FAIRY TRAIL

Help Petal follow the butterflies through the flower meadow,
flying from flower to flower in the order shown.
She can fly up, down, left, and right, but not diagonally.

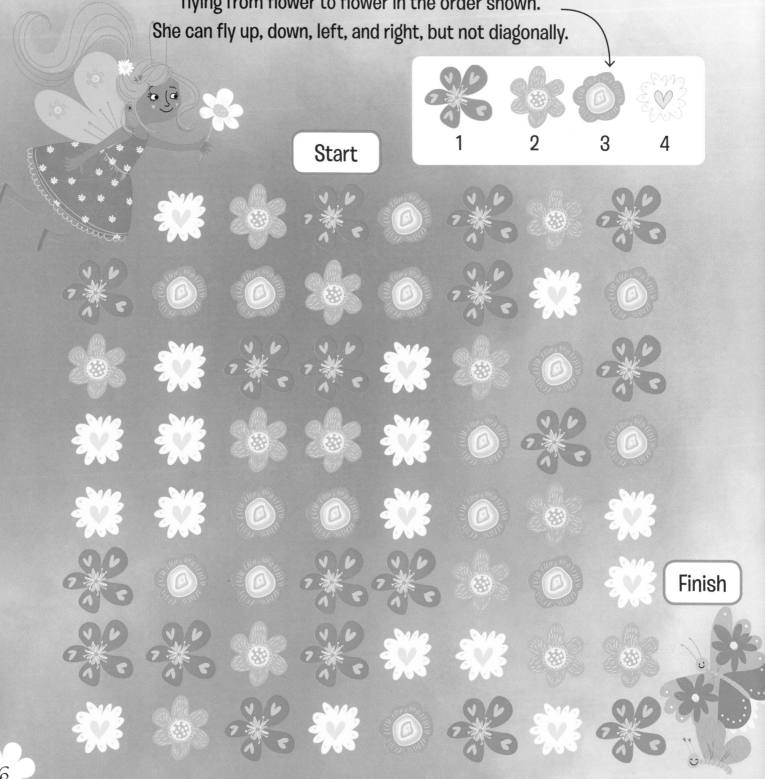

Start

Finish

Maze Fun

Can you help Candy find her way to the pink castle?

Start

Finish

Copy Cat

Carefully copy this picture of Rosebud and her pet kitten Bella
using the grid below to help you.

Party Treats

Bluebell has made a list of all the tasty treats she wants for her party.
Can you find the words in the grid below?

CUPCAKES **BROWNIES** **BANANAS** **ICE CREAM**
COOKIES **LEMONADE** **SANDWICHES** **STRAWBERRIES**

S	A	N	D	W	I	C	R	O	N	S	I
T	D	E	M	L	E	M	O	N	A	D	E
R	E	S	S	T	R	A	W	B	R	E	C
A	I	C	E	C	R	E	A	M	M	B	C
W	I	C	H	E	S	A	N	D	A	R	C
B	L	C	O	O	K	I	E	S	C	O	U
E	E	A	B	E	R	R	I	S	A	W	P
R	M	B	A	N	A	N	A	S	A	N	C
R	O	N	S	A	D	U	P	C	A	I	A
I	N	M	A	K	E	S	R	R	I	E	K
E	A	O	S	E	B	R	O	W	A	S	E
S	A	N	D	W	I	C	H	E	S	S	S

Winter Wonderland

A blanket of snow has fallen in Magic Land.
Can you discover eight differences between these two icy scenes?

Pool Party

Look at this picture of the mermaids' pool party for two minutes, and then turn the page to answer the questions without looking back.

Pool Party

1. How many mermaids are wearing pink goggles?

2. What is the fairy giving one of the mermaids?

3. How many pink flamingo floats are there?

4. Which playful sea animal is in the picture?

5. How many mermaids are wearing sun hats?

6. One mermaid is wearing water wings—are they yellow or blue?

Fantastic Features

Let your imagination go wild and add magnificent tails and manes to these beautiful unicorns. Add as many ribbons and bows as you like.

FIND THE CROWN

Jasmine has lost her beautiful crown. Can you help her find it?
She needs to step from jewel to jewel in this order, but not diagonally.

Start

1 2 3

Finish

Birthday Surprise!

It's Primrose's birthday and all her fairy friends have brought her gifts.
Can you unscramble the letters to see what they have given her?

A
ATELOOCCH

B
REPEMFU

C
TELRABCE

D
SNOBBIR

E
GRIN

Best Unicorn Friends

Can you find the BFFs? They are the only
two unicorns with matching outfits.

5 x 3

15 + 4

16 + 4

Petal Problem

The fairies have been busy collecting beautiful flowers to make a garland for Bluebell.

Solve the problems on their bags to find the fairy who has collected the most flowers.

8 x 2

25 - 4

Garden Party

There's a fabulous garden party at the magical castle.
Look at this picture for two minutes, and then turn the
page to answer the questions without looking back.

Garden Party

1. What kind of cuddly toy has the purple flying fairy won?

2. Does the yellow fairy have a vanilla or chocolate ice cream cone?

3. Is the castle purple or pink?

4. What game are two of the unicorns playing?

5. There is a fairground ride in the distance. Is it a Ferris wheel or a roller-coaster?

Add Some Magic

Use your pens and pencils to brighten up this magical scene.

Your Unicorn Name?

Your birth month + your fave baby animal = your unicorn name!
For example, if you were born in June and like puppies, your
unicorn name is TWINKLY SUNSHINE. Write down yours below!

JANUARY	SPARKLY	JULY	SHINY
FEBRUARY	DIAMOND	AUGUST	RAINBOW
MARCH	CRYSTAL	SEPTEMBER	DREAMY
APRIL	GOLDEN	OCTOBER	TWIRLY
MAY	GLITTERY	NOVEMBER	CANDY
JUNE	TWINKLY	DECEMBER	SHIMMERY

PUPPY	SUNSHINE
KITTEN	STARLIGHT
DUCKLING	SUNFLOWER
LAMB	BUTTERCUP
PIGLET	PRINCESS
BUNNY	MOONBEAM
CHICK	FIREGLOW

My unicorn name is:

....

My friend's unicorn name is:

....

Star of the Selfie

Primrose has posted five photos of her friend Crystal that look identical.
Can you tell which is the odd one out?

HURRY HOME!

Millie is meeting her friends at the Enchanted Castle.
Can you help her find a way through the maze?

Start

Finish

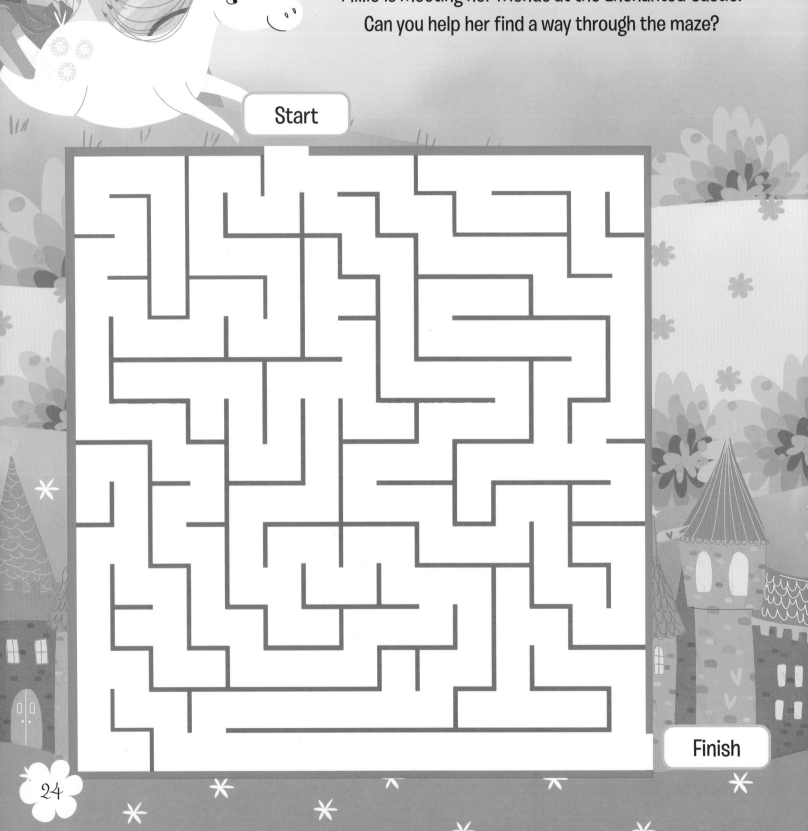

Unicorn Muddle

The unicorns have been playing at the beach with their pet sea creatures.
Can you follow the seaweed to see which creature belongs to each unicorn?

Dreamy Design

What do you think Petunia's dream castle looks like?
Decorate it with lots of pretty flowers and rainbows using your best pens and pencils.

Flower Show

Spring has sprung in Magic Land, and the fairies and unicorns are enjoying the displays. How many of each of these flowers can you see?

A   B   C   D

Magical Mall

It's a busy day at the magical mall. Look at the picture for two minutes, then turn the page to answer the questions without looking back.

Magical Mall

1. How many unicorns are in the picture?

2. There is a fairy trying on hats. Has she chosen a pink or green one?

3. What is the mermaid doing in the fountain?

4. Who is enjoying a milkshake with the fairies in the foreground, a mermaid or a unicorn?

5. What does the fairy statue have in her hands?

6. Does the unicorn having her hair styled have a yellow or blue mane?

Which Silhouette?

Which of these silhouettes is an exact match for Merry and her BFF Bella?

MERMAID ISLAND

Put this picture of Gabrielle and her mermaid friends back together.
Which piece doesn't fit anywhere?

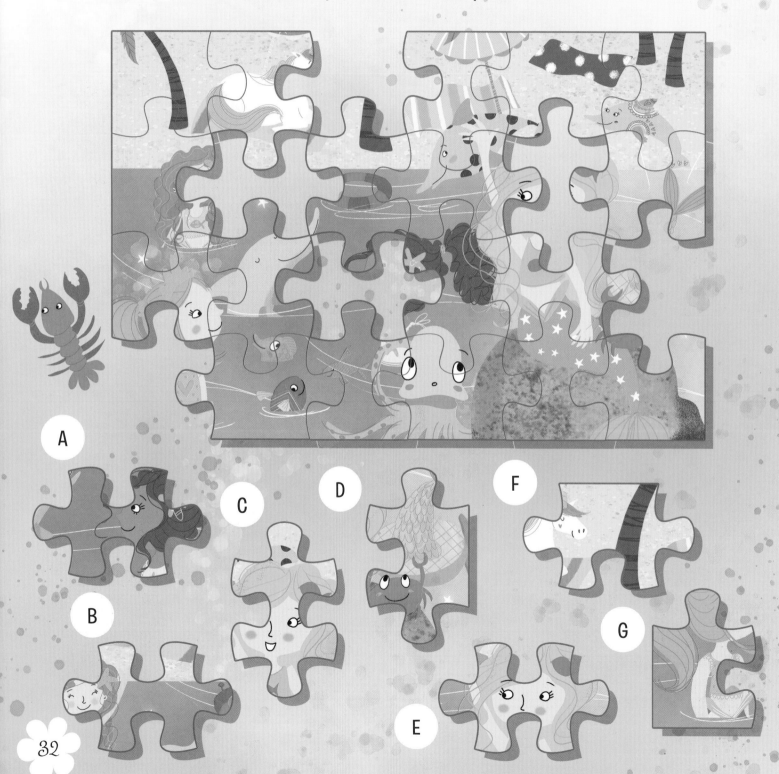

Pet Show

It's the annual pet show in Magic Land, and the unicorns are looking after their pets. Look at what they are holding, and figure out which pet belongs to each unicorn.

Paint the Meadow

Use your brightest pens and pencils to bring this unicorn scene to life.

Sleepover Code

Millie is having a sleepover party, and has sent a secret message to Primrose.
Can you figure out what it says?

GO	PLEASE	CUDDLY	YOUR
FIND	UNICORNS	THE	TO
BRING	TOWN	TOY	SLEEPOVER

Party Prep!

Melody is having a birthday party, and most of the guests have arrived.
Can you work out which sea creature is not there yet?

Turtle

Crab

Pink Fish

Green Fish

Seahorse

Sweet Tooth

No unicorn picnic would be complete without the fruits below.
Can you find them in the grid? The words can go forward, backward, or diagonally.

M	O	G	N	A	M	G	R	A	E	P	S
E	M	A	N	G	S	A	P	L	E	E	S
L	M	E	L	O	N	X	P	P	I	P	L
S	S	B	L	U	R	P	I	R	S	P	B
E	B	R	R	L	A	R	R	G	E	B	A
L	E	P	L	E	S	E	N	R	I	A	N
P	I	M	N	Y	B	R	O	A	R	N	A
P	E	I	R	W	L	R	A	P	R	N	N
A	P	M	A	R	U	A	L	E	E	L	A
S	A	R	S	S	B	P	P	S	H	L	S
P	T	I	R	R	E	S	I	A	C	N	N
S	E	I	R	R	E	B	E	U	L	B	S

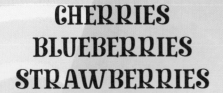

CHERRIES   MELON   PINEAPPLE
BLUEBERRIES   APPLES   MANGO
STRAWBERRIES   BANANAS   GRAPES

Draw Me

Follow the steps to create your own beautiful unicorn,
and then use your pens and pencils to make her pretty.

Find the Fairy

The fairies have hidden themselves around the magical castle.
Can you find all ten of them?

Meadow Fun

Can you find the unicorns below playing in the meadow?

Which one is missing?

A B C D E

Heads or Tails

Find a way from Sabrina's head to her tail, stepping on the horseshoes in this set order. She can move sideways, down, and up, but not diagonally.

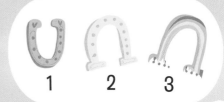

1   2   3

Start

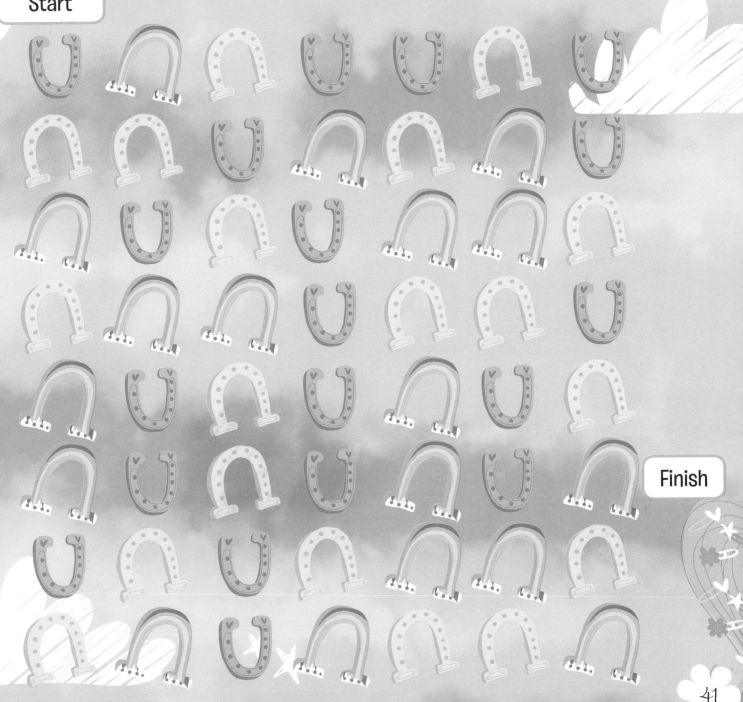

Finish

41

NATURE DAY

It's Nature Day in Magic Land, and the unicorns are out in the meadow,
hoping to spot a very rare lilac butterfly.
Can you help them find it?

Fill Them In

Can you draw in the missing lines on this unicorn?
Use your best pens and pencils and let your imagination run wild.

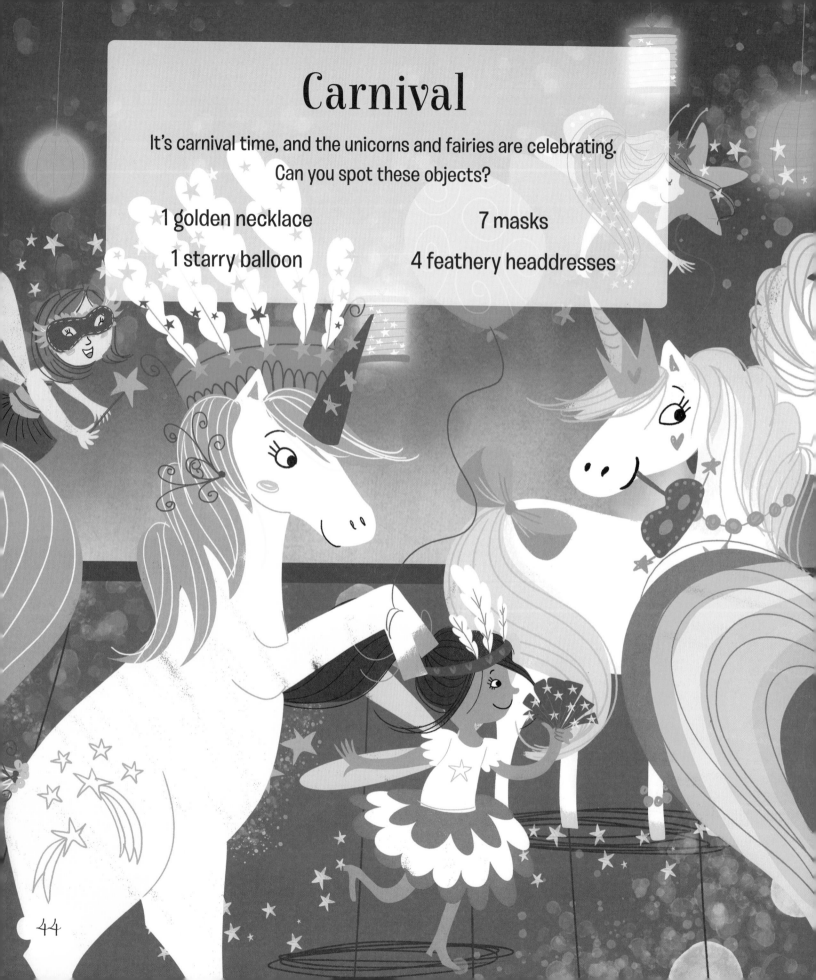

Carnival

It's carnival time, and the unicorns and fairies are celebrating.
Can you spot these objects?

1 golden necklace

1 starry balloon

7 masks

4 feathery headdresses

44

Whose Baby?

Which cute baby unicorn belongs to Millie?
Find the one whose numbers add up to the same number as hers.

A

$3 + 6 + 8 + 9 =$

B

$4 + 7 + 6 + 8 =$

$5 + 8 + 5 + 7 =$

C

$2 + 8 + 5 + 9 =$

INSTAGLAM!

Trixie is trying to decide which selfie she prefers.
They are all identical except for one. Can you figure out which one it is?

Seashell Necklace

Primrose wants to make a shell necklace with the most sparkle points for Sabrina, her unicorn bestie. Which group of shells should she choose?

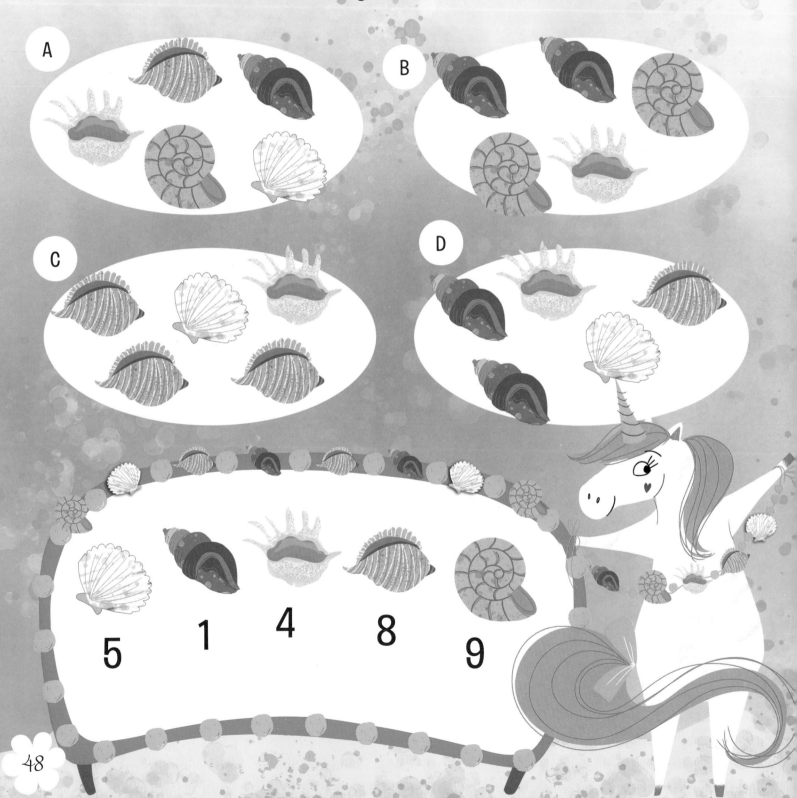

Spotty Dogs

The unicorns are exercising their new puppies.
Which of these cuties has the most spots?

SEASIDE FUN

It's a warm day in Magic Land, and the unicorns are down by the sea.
Which beach umbrella looks different from the rest?
How many sandcastles can you see?

50

Queen of the Sea

Ellie the unicorn will crown one of these mermaids Queen of the Sea. But which one? Solve the clues to see who it is.

1. Her hair is braided.

2. She's holding a comb.

3. Her shell necklace has blue beads.

Catch Me If You Can

The unicorns and fairies are playing tag in the meadow.
Can you fit the circles below into the scene? Which of the circles cannot be placed?

Winter Warmers

It's getting cold in Magic Land. The unicorns need their hats, mittens, and ear warmers, but they're all in a tangle. Can you follow the strings to figure out which item belongs to each unicorn?

Birthday Fun!

Luisa is having her quinceañera party. Study the picture for two minutes, then turn the page to answer the questions without looking back.

54

Birthday Fun!

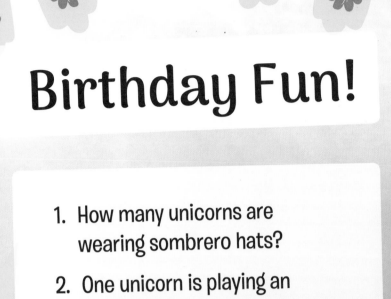

1. How many unicorns are wearing sombrero hats?

2. One unicorn is playing an instrument. Is it a horn or a guitar?

3. Which fairy is playing the red maracas?

4. What instrument is the green-haired fairy playing?

5. What is on top of the cake, a unicorn or a cactus?

Bake Me a Cake

The unicorns have baked a big cake for Serena's birthday.
Use your best pens and pencils to decorate it.

Mermaid Friends Forever

Serena and Melody are mermaid best friends.
Copy them into the grid below.

Daisy, Daisy

It's spring in Magic Land, and the fairies are making daisy chains for their unicorn friends.
Which fairy necklace contains the most flowers?

FIND THE HEADBAND

Millie can't find her special headband. It's the only one that doesn't have an exact match.

Sweet Delights

Sunbeam is off to collect honey from the rainbow bees, but she can only move from one flower to another in a set order. Can you help her by moving sideways, down, and up, but not diagonally?

Start

Finish

Spring Clean

It's time for a spring clean, and the fairies and unicorns like to share the chores.
Can you spot the eight differences between these two scenes?

Mermaid Feast

Mermaid princess Gabrielle is having a magical undersea feast, and she wants to invite her unicorn friends. Can you work out what she is serving for each course?

RIAFY   SKEAC

....

CHCOATLOE
PURRSSIE

....

....

YERRBWARTS
TRAT

....

....

Waterfall Diving

Which mermaid is best at waterfall diving?
Calculate who has the highest score to find out.

A

1/2 of 12 =

B

20 - 10 =

C

25 ÷ 5 =

Prom Pairs

It's the night of the Prom, and the fairies and unicorns are going together. Invent cute names for these unicorn and fairy best friends. Write them in the boxes below.

1

....

2

....

3

....

4

....

Whose Birthday?

Four unicorns have their birthdays on the same day,
and the equations on the cakes show their ages.
Which cake is for the oldest unicorn?

A

$$1/2 \text{ of } 18 =$$

B

$$21 - 10 =$$

C

$$2 \times 8 =$$

D

$$6 + 9 =$$

Nature Hunt

There are lots of creatures in Magic Land. Can you find their names hidden in the grid? The words can go forward or backward.

BUTTERFLY
HONEY BEE

BLUEBIRD
SQUIRREL

HEDGEHOG
WOODPECKER

B	U	T	T	E	F	Y	B	L	U	B	I
H	L	T	G	O	H	E	G	D	E	H	R
O	E	E	O	O	D	P	E	C	E	R	E
N	R	F	L	R	R	D	S	Q	U	I	K
E	R	B	U	T	T	E	R	F	L	Y	C
B	I	H	O	N	Y	B	E	B	L	I	E
B	U	W	O	O	D	P	E	B	E	A	P
E	Q	H	E	D	G	A	H	O	G	H	D
E	S	S	D	R	I	B	E	U	L	B	O
S	Q	U	I	R	R	A	L	H	E	D	O
H	O	N	E	Y	B	E	E	B	B	E	W
H	N	E	Y	B	I	R	B	L	U	W	O

FIND THE UNICORN

The unicorns are playing hide-and-seek, and have hidden in the forest.

Can you spot all ten of them?

Carnival Toys

These Magic Land friends have each won a cuddly toy at the carnival, but whose is whose? Follow the ribbons to find out.

Prom Puzzle

One of these unicorns will be made Prom Queen.
Solve the clues to see who it is.

1. She has yellow stars on her flank.

2. She is wearing a saddle.

3. Her mane is not braided.

Spooky Magic!

It's Halloween in Magic Land. Can you find 11 pumpkins hiding in the meadow? How many unicorns are playing trick or treat?

Festive Fun

The unicorns love getting ready for Christmas.
Can you spot these objects in this festive scene?

8 presents

2 stripy Christmas hats

3 pink heart decorations

6 candy canes

Secret Password

Serena has forgotten the secret password that lets her into the undersea castle.
Can you unscramble the letters so she can get inside?
It's the name of a sea creature.

TRASSHIF

....

Forest Friends

Can you put the pieces of this magical woodland scene back together?
Which piece doesn't belong at all?

Shell Puzzle

Fiona needs to find a way across Sea Shell Beach to join the fairies. She has to step on the shells in a set order. She can go up, down, left, and right, but not diagonally.

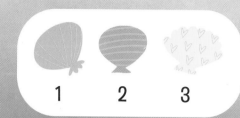

1   2   3

Start

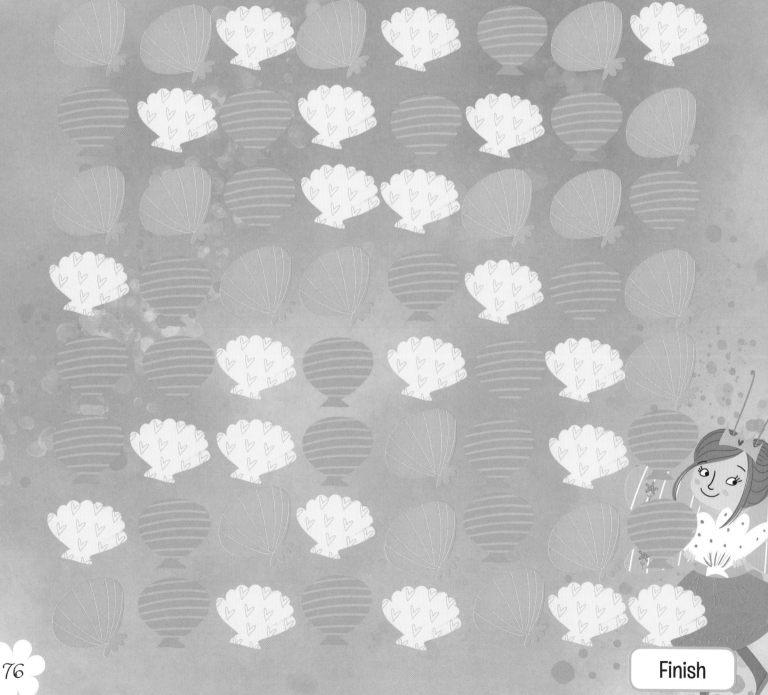

Finish

Dress Code

Petal is having a party and has left a special coded message for her best friend Primrose.
Can you figure out what she wants to tell her?

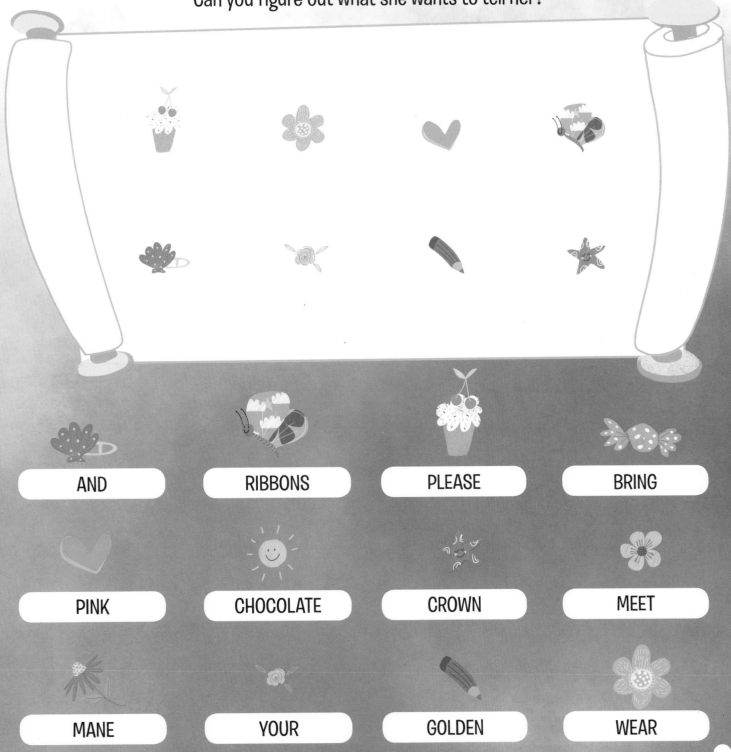

AND

RIBBONS

PLEASE

BRING

PINK

CHOCOLATE

CROWN

MEET

MANE

YOUR

GOLDEN

WEAR

77

FAIRY QUEEN

Bring this magical fairy scene to life using your best pens and pencils!

Twins Teaser

The unicorns and fairies are playing in the meadow.
But can you tell which two unicorns are identical twins?

What's in a Name?

Find the set of letters that can be unscrambled to spell the word UNICORN.

1 NORCCINU

2 ORRCINNU

3 CINONUR

4 CINUROM

5 INNUCOOR

Find the Teddy Bear

Ellie the baby unicorn has been playing in the meadow, but now it's bedtime and she can't find her special bear. Can you help her?

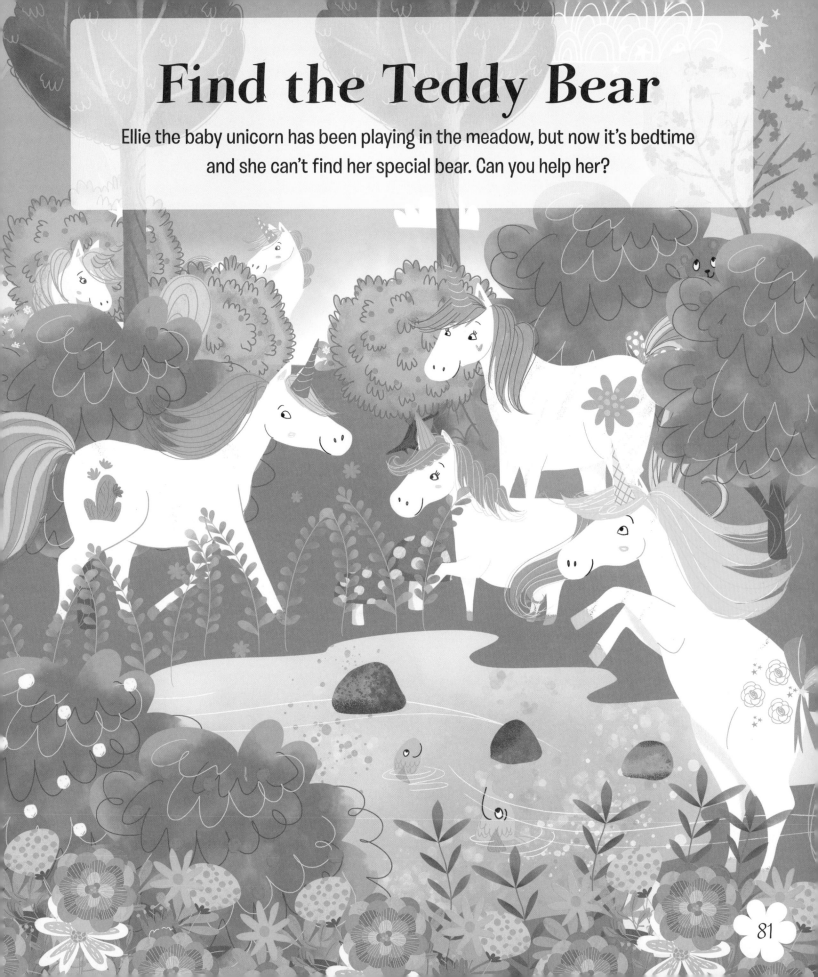

Bake Sale

The unicorns have been baking special treats.
Can you see which plate of the delicious treats below is NOT in the scene?

A

B

C

D

E

F

Which Wand?

Petal can't find her special wand. Can you help her?
It's the only one that doesn't have an exact match ...
and she's not already holding it.

Perfect Finish

Use your best pens and pencils to add magical manes and tails to these beautiful unicorns. Add cute patterns and bows!

Water Fun!

It's summer in Magic Land, so the unicorns are watering the flowers in the castle garden. Can you find the special flower with six petals?

SWEET SUDOKU

Fill in the blanks so that each row, column, and mini-grid has one of each type of delicious treat.

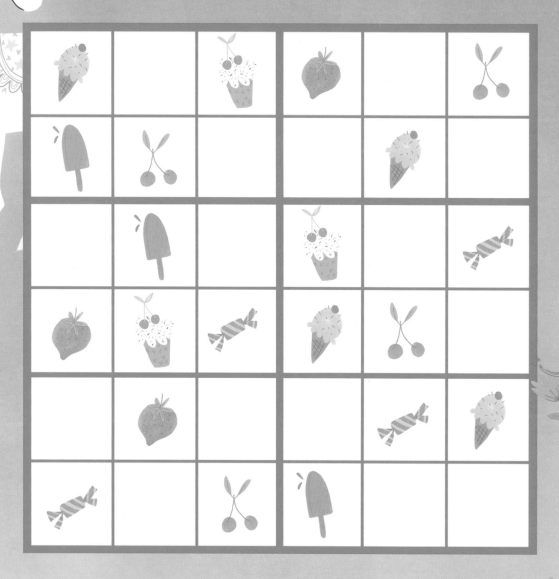

A

B

C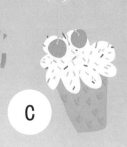

D

E

F

TIME FOR BED

Shh! The unicorns are fast asleep, but which unicorn is dreaming of a magic castle in the clouds?

87

Draw Your Unicorn Friend

What would your unicorn friend look like? What is her name?

Answers

Page 3

Page 4

Page 5

Piece E doesn't fit anywhere.

Page 6

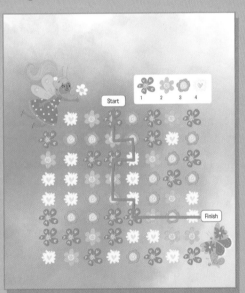

Page 7

Page 9

S	A	N	D	W	I	C	R	O	N	S	I
T	D	E	M	L	E	M	O	N	A	D	E
R	E	S	S	T	R	A	W	B	R	E	C
A	I	C	E	C	R	E	A	M	M	B	C
W	I	C	H	E	S	A	N	D	A	R	C
B	L	C	O	O	K	I	E	S	C	O	U
E	E	A	B	E	R	R	I	S	A	W	P
R	M	B	A	N	A	N	A	S	A	N	C
R	O	N	S	A	D	U	P	C	A	I	A
I	N	M	A	K	E	S	R	R	I	E	K
E	A	O	S	E	B	R	O	W	A	S	E
S	A	N	D	W	I	C	H	E	S	S	S

Page 10

89

Answers

Pages 11-12

1. Two mermaids are wearing pink goggles.
2. An ice cream cone.
3. There are five flamingo floats.
4. A dolphin.
5. Three mermaids are wearing sun hats.
6. Her water wings are yellow.

Page 14

Page 15

A = CHOCOLATE

B = PERFUME

C = BRACELET

D= RIBBONS

E = RING

Page 16

Page 17

Pages 18-19

1. A cuddly unicorn.
2. She has a big vanilla ice cream cone.
3. The castle is purple.
4. They are playing badminton.
5. A Ferris wheel.

Page 23

Answers

Page 24

Page 25

Page 27

YELLOW DAFFODILS = 3

PINK TULIPS = 4

RED ROSES = 2

SUNFLOWERS = 5

Pages 28-30

1. There are nine unicorns.

2. She has chosen a pink one.

3. Washing her hair.

4. A unicorn.

5. She is holding wands.

6. The unicorn has a blue mane.

Page 31

Page 32

Piece E doesn't fit anywhere.

Page 33

1 = Goldfish

2 = Puppy

3 = Hamster

4 = Budgie

5 = Kitten

Page 35

The secret code is:
PLEASE BRING YOUR CUDDLY TOY TO THE SLEEPOVER

Page 36

Turtle hasn't arrived yet.

Answers

Page 37

M	O	G	N	A	M	G	R	A	E	P	S
E	M	A	N	G	S	A	P	L	E	E	S
L	M	E	L	O	N	X	P	P	I	P	L
S	S	B	L	U	R	P	I	R	S	P	A
E	B	R	R	L	A	R	R	G	E	B	N
L	E	P	L	E	S	E	N	R	I	A	N
P	I	M	N	Y	B	R	O	A	R	N	A
P	E	I	R	W	L	R	A	P	R	N	N
A	P	M	A	R	U	A	L	E	E	L	A
S	A	R	S	S	B	P	P	S	H	L	S
P	T	I	R	R	E	S	I	A	G	N	N
S	E	I	R	R	E	B	E	U	L	B	S

Page 40

Page 42

Page 39

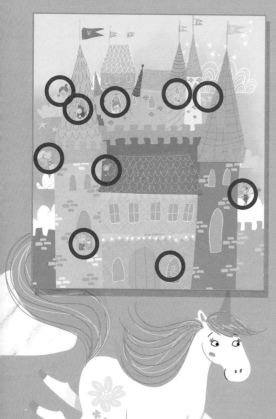

Page 41

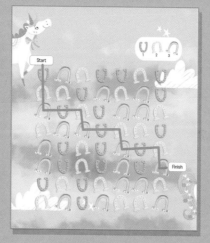

Pages 44-45

Answers

Page 46

Millie's number is 25 and her baby unicorn is B.

A = 3 + 6 + 8 + 9 = 26

B = 4 + 7 + 6 + 8 = 25

C = 2 + 8 + 5 + 9 = 24

Page 47

Page 48

Answer C.

A = 27

B = 24

C = 33

D = 19

Page 49

Page 50

Page 51

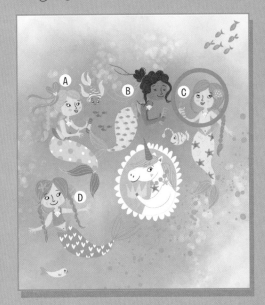

Page 52

Piece D cannot be placed.

Answers

Page 53

Pages 54-55

1. Two unicorns are wearing sombreros.
2. The unicorn is playing a guitar.
3. The one with blue hair.
4. She is playing a horn.
5. A cactus is on top of the cake.

Page 59

Answer is Fairy C with 6 flowers on her chain.

Page 60

Page 61

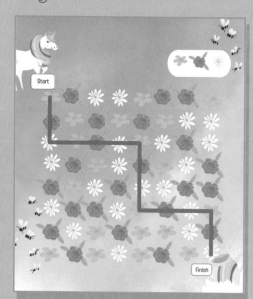

Page 62

Page 63

FAIRY CAKES

CHOCOLATE SURPRISE

STRAWBERRY TART

Page 64

The answer is B.

A. 1/2 of 12 = 6

B. 20 - 10 = 10

C. 25 ÷ 5 = 5

Page 66

The answer is C.

A. 1/2 of 18 = 9

B. 21 - 10 = 11

C. 3 x 8 = 16

D. 7 + 9 = 15

Page 67

B	U	T	T	E	F	Y	B	L	U	B	I
H	L	T	G	O	H	E	G	D	E	H	R
O	E	E	O	O	D	P	E	G	E	R	E
N	R	F	L	R	R	D	S	Q	U	I	K
E	R	B	U	T	T	E	R	F	L	Y	G
B	I	H	O	N	Y	B	E	B	L	I	E
B	U	W	O	O	D	P	E	B	E	A	P
E	Q	H	E	D	G	A	H	O	G	H	D
E	S	S	D	R	I	B	E	U	L	B	O
S	Q	U	I	R	R	A	L	H	E	D	O
H	O	N	E	Y	B	E	E	B	B	E	W
H	N	E	Y	B	I	R	B	L	U	W	O

Answers

Page 68

Page 69

Page 70

Answer = C

Page 71

Three unicorns are playing trick or treat.

Page 74

The secret password is:

STARFISH

Page 72-73

Page 75

Piece B doesn't belong.

Page 76

Answers

Page 77

The coded message is:
PLEASE WEAR PINK RIBBONS
AND YOUR GOLDEN CROWN

Page 79

Unicorns 1 and 5 are twins.

Page 80

Answer = 3

Page 81

Page 82

Page 83

Page 85

Page 86

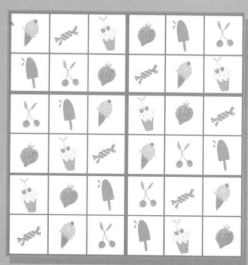

Page 87